HACKER POLITICS

REVOLUTION & DEMOCRACY 2.0

DEREK FLETCHER

HACKER POLITICS

REVOLUTION & DEMOCRACY 2.0

COPYRIGHT

© 2018 Derek Fletcher

Independently Published

ISBN: 9781976853883

THIS BOOK IS DEDICATED TO:

This book is dedicated to all of the men and women who have contributed to trying to make this American experiment with democracy a successful one. Efforts which no matter their present outward expressions have been birthed through one quintessential American spirit…revolution.

THIS PAGE INTENTIONALLY LEFT BLANK

CONTENTS

INTRODUCTION

I have been asked why I decided to write this book. My general response to this question is "force." In my estimation, one does not decide to write a book of this sort but rather is moved to do so. In my particular case, the force of which I speak was the force of my conscience. Even the most strong willed person is powerless against resisting a conscience that disturbs his every waking hour as well as his sleep. Perhaps it would be insightful to add a little texture to my personal experience.

Anyone who has decided to write a book, and actually completes it, can tell you there are significant challenges. Though there are many genres of writing, the completion of such a process, is on the whole quite taxing. One needs the requisite time and environment to develop the content, organize it and then begin writing. This effort alone can take weeks, months or years depending on the subject matter, its depth and the intended audience. If I were to describe my experience in two words they would be "exhausting" and "exhilarating."

This book required a couple of years of "field work." I am not a technical professional or engineer so I had to spend some time in the company and environment of those who are. Once I made the decision, I packed my belongings and headed to Silicon Valley in Northern California. I attended events, conferences and public discourses in the Valley and San Francisco. I also read magazines, periodicals and books prominent in the tech field at the time. Free online courses in basic physics and computer programming were also useful. The most valuable experiences were the direct engagements in conversations with members of the tech community. All of this while keeping a mindful eye on the volatile political landscape.

I had a small technical project that I was able to use as a talking piece and a way to gain some potential insight into a world in which I was clearly an outsider. Having this project in hand allowed me to also apply what I was learning. I found, more often than not, that the community freely engaged with me. I was told this was so because "I was a good thinker" and asked "good questions."

The engineering community is (as of this writing) quite insular and predominately male. Most seemed to prefer the company of other engineers as they were likely to share a common interest, mode of communication and lifestyle. My philosophical mind and ability to use logic effectively is what gave me a "pass." Nor at any time did I pretend to be an engineer or aspire to be one. I believe that authenticity was appreciated. My goal was merely to observe and reflect.

I recall the first few times (in the open public) that I heard the word "hacker" being used. Initially, I thought to myself I have no intentions of socializing with hackers. At that time, my knowledge of that word only conjured up thoughts related to criminal activity. I had difficulty reconciling my notions of a hacker and how the word was being used by some engineers and technical professionals from top universities and global companies. One chapter in this book, "Enter The

Hacker," will help the reader develop a clearer understanding of the use of the word hacker in various contexts.

I am a voracious reader. I am particularly fond of philosophy, biographies, spiritual writings and also theoretical thought in the physical and social sciences. I enjoy rigorous analysis and employing an immense imaginative energy towards these subjects. But, this activity, while thoroughly enjoyable to me, would be an utter waste of life if I did not try to use it for meaningful purposes. To me, that means trying to live more consciously as well as seeking ways to improve society and relieve the suffering of others. Many philosophers and theorists today feel no sense of this while others simply feel it is not their place to act in such a role.

Over the course of my life, I have read many books, essays and works of some of the greatest minds in western culture who have written on political philosophy and theory. Some of these individuals include John Locke, Thomas Hobbes, Plato, Karl Marx and Aristotle. Others were Jean-Jacques Rousseau, John Stuart Mill, Cicero, Montesquieu, Niccolo Machiavelli and Thomas Paine. The Federalist Papers, Edict Of Nantes, Magna Carta, United States Constitution and writings of historically prominent Americans (including the founding members) have also been very insightful.

When one actively and critically engages with so many towering intellects possessing such divergent points of view, he cannot but reflect upon his own country. This becomes especially so when the nation shaped and molded by these minds is willingly falling short of even the least of these ideals. Presently, in America, political discourse has collapsed into mere personal attack, orchestrated pageantry and buffoonery. Instead of turning to serious individuals of erudition, wisdom and depth there is a reliance opinion polls and the chatter of those more expert in entertainment and recreation rather than important matters of statehood. Popularity is favored over discernment and experience even when electing individuals to city, state or federal positions.

While this dreadful reality is not solely responsible for all of the government's shortcomings it goes a long way in expediting this nation's decline. The possibility that this nation will be destroyed militarily by another nation is presently unlikely. No, what is more likely is that this nation will self destruct or implode (as several previous powerful nations have done) thereby making itself vulnerable to attack by any country who may seek to do it harm. The political and social antagonism between citizens, and between the government and citizens, is at a level that makes the 1960's look tamed.

America has many great qualities. One of its best qualities is the ability to articulate the highest ideals as they relate to self government and statehood. However, the visions of America articulated by the revolutionary founding members of this nation have not been fully realized. That said, it would be untrue to state that there has not been any progress from their day to ours. Indeed there has been much progress. However, there are two areas in which this nation has moved so far in the wrong direction that the revolutionary founding members might not even believe they were walking on American soil if present today.

America is failing in these two areas. One, in its unrestricted surveillance and hacking of innocent citizens. Second, in the initiation of, and participation in, wars and armed conflicts under dubious and or false pretenses. The chapter, "Transparency As A Right" explores this thought in more detail. It was the contemplation of these two problems, coupled with the desire to seek a revolutionary way to remedy them, that led to the writing of this book.

Today, the government is completely suspicious of its citizens. Anyone in public who can so much as pronounce a two syllable word with proper diction can become a "person of interest." Likewise, unlike the revolutionary days of early America, citizens are deeply afraid of the government rather than government respecting an honoring its citizens. The source of this suspicion and fear is rooted in distrust. Somehow, America has turned against itself.

The two most important components of any stable nation are a healthy relationship between its citizens and government and secondly respect for the laws that govern this relationship. But these two components are buttressed by something far more fundamental, namely trust. Without a fundamental and genuine trust between these parties the downward trajectory, accompanying violence and general discord we daily witness will become the rule rather than the exception. Hope will not deliver us from this challenge. Only reasoned revolutionary political action will change this situation.

In my estimation, a solution to these two problems does not require overthrowing the existing government. This is not 18th century America. Our time, and theirs, are not wholly analogous. But, the values of justice, and a right to privacy that inspired their actions, ought inspire ours today. The weightiness of all of this on my conscience would not let me rest until I made some overt attempt to address these problems. I attempted to push it aside. I tried not to let the political apathy and cynicism I felt to stifle my responsibility as a citizen to initiate a public dialogue about these problems. These two problems negatively impact every American and only result in greater animosity and distrust.

Party and identity politics will mean nothing if the nation cannot remain intact. Every day I see Americans willing to attack each other over ideological and sociological differences. One must either be a liberal or conservative, left or right…a donkey or an elephant. All the while Americans are engaged in these side disputes the inalienable rights guaranteed under the laws of this nation are being eroded. There is no conspiracy on the part of the government. No, rather it's the emphasis and scrutiny on lesser disputes between fellow citizens and the lack of such attention on government actions that is preventing us from addressing the domestic threats and harm to this nation's highest values.

There is no glory, acclaim or accolades to be had for submitting this discussion to the public for debate. In fact, in today's climate of division, separation and suspicion I run the risk of ridicule and scorn rather than praise. Praise or scorn, I had no choice but to present it. Perhaps there are those who can stand outside and idly watch a house burn to the ground without attempting to throw at least one bucket of water on the blaze. I am not one of them…

Derek Fletcher

DESIGNING DEMOCRACY

Our cruel and unrelenting Enemy leaves us no choice but a brave resistance, or the most abject submission; this is all we can expect - We have therefore to resolve to conquer or die: Our own Country's Honor, all call upon us for a vigorous and manly exertion, and if we now shamefully fail, we shall become infamous to the whole world.

~George Washington, Revolutionary & First President of The United States of America

When a team sets out to design a product there are some general principles of organization and procedure that must be agreed upon before the actual design process begins. Invariably, any member of a design team may think his or her role in the design process is worthy of the most attention. One charged with responsibility for the aesthetic design of the product will quarrel with another responsible for meeting the required release date. Both of these individuals may argue with the person responsible for staying within the assigned budget for the project. Anyone who has worked on the design of a project, or even planning an event, knows that the moment other people get involved there must be compromise.

Designing America's brand of democracy is an immensely complex process. This product's design has been written not only in words, symbols and ideas but also in blood. Unlike designing other products, merely to be sold in the market, America's democracy has not completely dispensed with its obsolete legacy components. (e.g. racism, bigotry, chauvinism etc) This is primarily due to the fact that this obsolescence is carried forward in the culture, minds and hearts of people. People are the only reason why government emerges. Trying to get thousands, or now millions, of citizens to agree on what American democracy should look like today seems impossible. Yet, that is the task as it was for the generations that preceded us.

It needs to be understood that this design process is never finished. There is not a point where Americans should leave this matter in the "hands of government" to workout and then resort to protesting about the negative results of personal neglect. Sadly, today this is what too many American citizens believe to be the extent of their civic duty. Vote for candidates who are the least repulsive among a group of undesirables and then protest the chaos that results from their decisions and policies. Americans present involvement in designing America's democracy is as a spectator. Democracy is happening to them, not for them. This was not the intention of founding members of this country.

This is not a history book. There are plenty of books written about the American Revolution. The Intolerable Acts (also called Coercive Acts in Britain), Boston Tea Party, Stamp Act and similar historical events provide ample reasons for the causes of the American Revolution. One would be wise to read or revisit that literature after finishing this book. One is clearly able to see the difference between the mindset of citizens who were designing their democracy compared to the more passive posture taken today by too many Americans.

In American democracy 1.0, the notion of government of the people by the people had a completely different meaning than it does today. Those Americans would undoubtedly be considered "persons of interest" by this government. Why? Their understanding and expression of designing democracy was bound to a revolutionary spirit. They were willing to give their lives for the sake of American democracy. Make no mistake about this, they were not required to do this but chose to. They could have simply continued to submit to tyrannical rule and unjust abuses. But, they knew that once the mind and heart becomes steadied by greater principles such as justice and freedom, that fear could not be allowed to prevail over what was at stake.

American democracy1.0 (here-forward Ad1) required blood shed and war. But for the sacrifices of life and limb made by those individuals, the rights guaranteed under the United States Constitution cherished by many today would not exist. These were not bloodthirsty individuals who craved war. They simply had to resort to an effective design tool preserved only for the deepest threats to citizen freedoms and rights. That tool is revolution. Many Americans today are afraid of the word. Frankly, to fear this word as an American, is to display a lack of knowledge and understanding of American history. This unwarranted fear also severs one from the spirit that ought to inspire every American's sense of civic duty.

But, it may be asked what makes an act revolutionary? What is its criteria? How can it be distinguished from mere irrational passions or misguided delusions? This is a great question. The answer is clear and supported by this nation's own beginnings and subsequent development.

As I see it, a revolutionary act must have several components to legitimately qualify as such. One, the act must be directed towards one's own established government or nation. Second, it must be initiated and carried out exclusively by citizens of that nation. Third, the act must be initiated for legitimate political purposes. Fourth, the act must be executed exclusively utilizing domestic resources. Fifth, it should always be used defensively never offensively.

Revolutionary acts must be directed towards one's own government or nation

Today, acts of aggression are carried out by citizens of one nation against governments and nations not their own. This is most exemplified by the global terrorist activities. People living under oppressive regimes and governments attack other countries whom they believe are either entirely responsible for their oppression or at least share culpability sufficient to warrant attacking them. These types of attacks by individuals or groups cannot even be classified as acts of war let alone revolution. Legitimate acts of war must be declared and executed by a government or nation against another sovereign nation. Terrorism is its own class of unjustifiable violence.

Given the volatility and instability that revolutionary activity may potentially cause, it ought not be initiated simply to settle ideological differences between political parties or competing factions. Today, in America, Democrats and Republicans, conservatives, progressives and liberals are teeming with hostilities. Increasingly, these differences are leading to violence. This behavior, repugnant in and of itself, would become unforgivable if any of these groups attempted to justify their violence under the false pretense of legitimate revolutionary action.

Revolutionary acts must be initiated and carried out exclusively by citizens

Revolutionary activity is a private national matter with potentially international impact. The reasons for engaging in such activity must be home grown. History has shown us that nations often initiate, cause or otherwise support civil wars and coups in other countries for completely self-serving reasons. That these same nations often try to either deny or hide their activity is evidence of ulterior motives. Revolutionary activity is solely the business of a nation's citizens.

They alone will be directly left with the immediate aftermath of this activity. Language, history, culture, social norms and existing circumstances within a nation are all organic ingredients that shape legitimate revolutionary activity.

Once other nations or governments inject their artificial "assistance" into revolutionary activity, it can lead to several catastrophic outcomes. It could unnecessarily prolong the activity. It could result in an outcome worse than the present situation. It could be manipulated into an excuse for assisting nations to escalate conflicts, between themselves, completely unrelated to the grievances for which the citizens are seeking relief. The nation could become a target for a dictator or despot. Precious resources and materials can be looted by the assisting nations. Lastly, the assisting nation may negotiate or require that its assistance is contingent upon agreement to terms that would prove detrimental or oppressive to the native country.

Revolutionary acts must be initiated for legitimate political purposes

Greed, jealousy, envy and poor reasoning has created a lot of hostility between foes and friends alike. As common as these feelings may be, they could not be used to justify revolutionary activity. Legitimate political purposes include holding the government to rights already guaranteed under current law. It can be employed to prevent the government from committing the country (including its resources) to causes and wars which the majority of the people do not agree. For more examples, review the myriad reasons that led up to the American Revolution like taxation without representation. They would also qualify as legitimate political purposes for revolutionary activity.

Revolutionary acts must be executed exclusively utilizing domestic resources

If citizens of a nation choose to engage in revolutionary activity, they must absorb any of the consequences of that activity. They should not expect another nation to suffer any losses in furtherance of revolutionary activity not executed on their home soil. This requirement forces several considerations. One, it gives citizens additional incentive to consider whether revolutionary activity is truly the solution to their current grievances. They will have to consider all of the legal rights and resources, should there be any, presently available to them "at home."

Next, given no support will come from the outside to aid citizens' efforts, it gives reason a greater chance to play a role in the execution of any revolutionary activity. Time has a way of taming passion. Lastly, it may eliminate, or significantly reduce, the use of violence as a means of revolutionary activity. Only those really committed to certain principles are likely to be willing to engage in an activity when their defeat is more likely than not. Most people are not this courageous even when subjected to great injustices.

Revolutionary acts should always be used defensively and not offensively

Read through the history of revolutionary acts and one will find at least one common characteristic. That common characteristic is that the activity is always illegal. But, this fact is perfectly consistent with reason. No government has, or would, give its citizens the right to force changes in its behavior outside of any legal or legislative processes it has created for those purposes. Many governments (sadly including US) view themselves in a paternalistic relationship with their citizens. In their eyes, giving citizens any such right would only invite anarchy and chaos.

While revolutionary activity is de facto illegal, this should never be a reason to avoid or abandon its consideration. However, it should raise in the minds of citizens the seriousness of such activity. It ought to cause them to ask themselves if the nature of the abuse or harms they seek to correct are commensurate with the seriousness of severing the social contract it has with the government and other citizens who may be opposed to revolutionary activity. This is a particularly important consideration when the government is a stable one. This is also why revolutionary activity, to be legitimate, should be defensive. Revolutionary activity is a shield not a sword. The specific issue of violence as a means of revolutionary activity is addressed in the third chapter.

Fearing the notion, or practice, of revolutionary political acts is antithetical to the American democratic ethos. Revolutionary spirit is responsible for building this nation. It is what emboldened men and women to attempt an experiment of self government unprecedented in western culture up until that time. What made this revolutionary activity remarkable was not bloodshed or war. The least intelligent among us can engage in violence without principles or moral purpose. No, what made this particular revolutionary experiment exceptional was the design concept upon which it was founded.

The more palpable way of stating this concept is "government of the people by the people." Their revolutionary spirit is what gave birth and meaning to this important design concept. Having been on the receiving end of abuse by government, the founding members of America envisioned a country where their government would have to give serious consideration about the repercussions of trampling over the rights of citizens. Americans were particularly on guard about any abuses related to personal privacy, property, freedom of speech and taxes.

Two amendments to the US Constitution, the second and fourth, were crafted specifically to protect citizens from abusive government action. In ignorance, today many arguments are advanced regarding the reason the right to bear arms was written into the Second Amendment. The language of the

Second Amendment reads: "A well regulated Militia, being necessary to the security of a free State, the right of the people to bear arms shall not be infringed." It has nothing to do with hunting or culture. Its original intent was strictly personal and political. They wanted guns for personal protection. But, they also wanted the newly formed government to ever be on notice that any blatant attempts at abusing their rights would be met with resistance.

In 2008, the United States Supreme Court recognized the right to bear arms for personal security inside the home in District of Columbia et al. v. Heller. That case held, "The Second Amendment protects an individual right to possess a firearm unconnected with service in a militia, and to use that arm for traditionally lawful purposes, such as self defense within the home." In 2010, the Supreme Court held that state and federal governments must comply with the right to bear arms for self defense purposes in McDonald et al v. City of Chicago, Illinois. To clarify, my interpretation of the Second Amendment, and these cases, is that the right to bear arms does not authorize one to unilaterally nullify or otherwise invalidate established laws. It is a defensive protection for self defense purposes against personal attack by criminals or government.

The Fourth Amendment was created to protect citizens from unreasonable searches and seizures. Americans had first hand experience, under British rule, with the indignities associated with unfettered government intrusion. The language of the Fourth Amendment reads: "The right of the people to be secure in their persons, houses, papers, and effects, against unreasonable searches and seizures, shall not be violated, and no Warrants shall issue, but upon probable cause, supported by Oath or affirmation, and particularly describing the place to be searched and the persons or things to be seized." The Patriot Act, 2008 Amendments to the Foreign Intelligence Surveillance Act of 1978 and activities of the National Security Agency have virtually voided the protections of the 4th Amendment.

Blatant abuse of citizens's rights is destructive to a nation, but add to this perpetual war and the collapse of a nation accelerates tenfold. Some have argued that war stimulates the economy and creates jobs. While this argument is not entirely fallacious, it perfectly illustrates an unscrupulous penchant for war. Likewise, whatever economic stimulation it may create, the actual overall costs emotionally, psychologically, spiritually and politically are negative. Yet America spends an unbelievable amount of its total funds on war and war related activities.

Today, American democracy faces a significant challenge. The government has been able to simultaneously trample upon citizen rights as well as act contrary to their best interest when expedient to do so. Lack of attention has put citizens in a precarious situation whereby reason alone may not rescue them. A government accustomed to abusing its power, and the public trust, is unlikely to willingly cease that activity. Citizen silence or ignorance of the activity is only incentive for the abuse to continue.

Ad1 involved a conflict with an external threat. In American democracy 2.0, the problem is internal. While acts of terrorism are serious and need to be combated, no amount of terrorism will destroy America's democracy faster than a government that has run amok. Terrorism has the power to draw more attention because it's violent. Explosions, mass shootings and similar violent acts have imagery that when broadcasted 24 hours a day on the news results in Americans believing that terrorism is the greatest threat. Physical threats, close or remote, stir up a sense of anxiety and immediate concern in the human psyche.

On the other hand, bad government action raises no concern until it's discovered. Often times it is never discovered.

Bad government acts impact the nation like a cancer does the body. It often has already done irreversible damage by the time it is detected. In light of the information learned through whistleblowers, Edward Snowden and digital publishers like WikiLeaks, we can no longer naively disbelieve what many Americans have long suspected is in fact happening.

The government has gone far beyond the bounds of protecting the privacy of innocent Americans into becoming the chief violator of this right. There is no sense of remorse or wrongdoing for these abuses on behalf of the government. Likewise, anyone who exposes proof of this horrific behavior by the government is treated harshly. We should note that when such information is released to the American public the government does not respond with "we did not do it." It responds with labeling whistleblowers as traitors and guilty of treason.

Government officials say that whistleblowers release information in violation of their employment agreement or that they must have some ulterior motives for having openly exposed this bad government action. This pitiful defense, if it may be called a defense, is a far cry from acknowledging its wrongdoing. Once any allegations of anti-patriotism are injected into the matter, the government knows the issue is on its way to the graveyard to be forgotten. Dear reader, this is the state of American democracy. America has cancer. Whether it becomes terminal is up to you.

In some ways, the task is significantly more complex and challenging than it was for our predecessors. This is not simply red coats versus blue coats. Nor can the government be seen as an enemy. The lines cannot be so clearly drawn in the sand. Nonetheless, we are not left to act completely in the blind. Today, there are more opportunities than in previous generations to re-establish citizen participation in designing America's democracy.

The task now is only to begin asking some very uncomfortable questions. We must begin to inquire about what is more important to us today. Does American democracy 2.0 require revolutionary solutions to save it? Who among us has the will, the skill and interest to raise these troubling questions to save this democracy? Are today's citizens simply just unworthy of this democracy left in their charge? While the condition is not yet terminal it can't be left to chance and one certainly can't hope that the government will suddenly cease to act counter to its present course of action. Let us now delve a bit more deeply into the nature of revolutionary activity from a classical perspective.

PORTRAIT OF CLASSICAL REVOLUTIONARY ACTIVITY

I know not what course others may take. But, as for me …
give me liberty or give me death!

~Patrick Henry, Revolutionary & Governor of Virginia

The word 'revolution' is one of the most politically charged words which can be publicly uttered by a citizen. To some, the word is inspirational and stirs up thoughts and emotions of a better tomorrow. For at least as many others, this word triggers fear, thoughts of unlawful violence and terror committed by hoodlums and criminals. I intend to paint a portrait of what I call the classical revolutionary. With this understanding in mind, we will be better prepared to deeply reflect upon, and debate, the provocative and controversial question raised by this book.

The word 'revolution' derives from the Latin word 're-volvere' which means 'to roll back.' It was first applied to the movement of celestial bodies. After the 14th century, it began to expand to mean 'an instance of great change in affairs.' Around the 16th century, the word began to take on the meaning most people assign to it today which is 'the overthrow of an existing political system or government.' A revolutionary is understood to be one who engages in the promotion or execution of a revolution.

How a revolution is viewed by people depends upon whether they support or oppose it. If they support it, the revolutionaries are called liberators, heroes, freedom fighters, or in America's case "founding fathers." Those who oppose the revolution will call those same individuals dissidents, traitors, rebels or insurgents. The opposition or status quo might also call revolutionaries terrorists. When a revolution ensues, the lines are drawn early and the use of language becomes a clear indicator of who its proponents and opponents are.

The reasons that give raise to the revolutionary impulse are many. Revolutionaries may emerge to prevent or correct injustices of government. These injustices may be real or perceived. Disagreement about the validity of the injustice fuels the revolutionary's course of action. Some of the common injustices that beckon revolutionaries involve the ownership of property, control of natural resources, differences in political ideology and the distribution or management of public goods and services. Revolutionary action may also be sparked by government abuse of citizens' rights.

Today, we can add another influence on revolutionary activity. It is the globalization and mutual interdependence of economic markets. This interdependence causes some governments to seek direct influence or control over other countries' political processes, military capabilities or natural resources. The typical reason given for these intrusions is that "it's in our country's national interests to do so." Under this foreign intrusion model, the revolutionary emerges not from an organic sense of injustice, but is incited by an external source of provocation with domestic repercussions.

ROLES

The potential role of revolutionaries vary depending on many factors. Heretofore, you may have been thinking of the revolutionary as a single person. Perhaps you had in mind that individual or personality associated with being the face of the revolution. Though almost every revolution has a main spokesperson, he or she is supported by a number of people that are also revolutionaries. We should not assume that the lack of co-revolutionaries' public appearance make them any less essential to the cause. In fact, the confidentiality of co-revolutionaries may be strategically necessary for success. We turn now to some of the roles of revolutionaries.

LEADER

Leaders in revolutions act similar to chief executive officers of an enterprise or a general in the military. They are charged with the overall direction of the cause and its execution. As such, few if any, are generally more committed to the cause than the leadership. One of the primary roles of a leader is as spokesperson to the public. These leaders usually receive a lot of public attention. This attention has a dual effect. It energizes members of the revolution because through the spokesperson they believe their voices are being heard. However, it simultaneously results in scorn, hatred and fear of the revolutionary by the opposition or status quo.

The revolutionary leader also has the main responsibility of articulating the positions and values of the revolution to the co-revolutionaries. It is essential to keep their morale up and reinforce the truth and validity of their cause. This is normally achieved through passionate speeches at gatherings, written communications such as pamphlets, newspapers, journals or fliers. Today, electronic and digital communications, e-mails and text messaging can also be used for these purposes. No matter the mode of communication employed, that communication needs to be meaningful and frequent enough to sustain the commitment of participants under difficult situations. This is the revolutionary as motivator.

Another crucial role for leaders in a revolution is that of legislator. Leaders are responsible for formalizing the philosophical, political, theoretical or spiritual platform of the revolution. Without clear and articulate unifying principles, co-revolutionaries may be easily dissuaded, scared or manipulated by the status quo. Sometimes a leader may craft a platform without the input from others. However, most often, other people are involved with platform development and may be partially responsible for its dissemination.

A leader in a revolution serves as judge among the group. They are charged not with executing punishment or discipline, but deciding if one ought to be punished or disciplined. A decision to discipline someone may be due to a failure to act in accordance with established values of the cause, a security breach, or disobeying the chain of command. In the role of judge, a leader also determines who should be praised, rewarded or honored. Regarding positive reinforcements, the leader often will personally execute or deliver that recognition. This builds additional loyalty with the recipient and encourages the group to act in good faith and in furtherance of the revolution.

Should a revolution reach a point where negotiation with the status quo is required, the lead revolutionary assumes the role of negotiator. In this role, a revolutionary must exercise tact and skill under extremely hostile or violent circumstances. Co-revolutionaries often expect their leader not to make compromises with the status quo. Many who feel this way fail to understand the necessity of being prepared to make concessions and compromises in order to achieve the ultimate objective of the cause. This anti-compromise sentiment stems from the risks they've taken to participate in the revolution.

Some of these risks may include being imprisoned, tortured, killed or financially ruined. It may also include death threats to loved ones or their actual demise. During negotiations, a revolutionary leader must successfully balance the demands of the status quo with that of the revolution's goals and aims. When the direction of an entire nation and the lives of many people are at stake, the ability to negotiate well cannot be overstated. Revolutions have lasted months or years in the past. They may at once appear to cease only to recommence with even greater fervor and commitment by its supporters. Quick and unforeseeable shifts in resources, allegiances and political winds all may also result in highly unpredictable negotiation tactics and results.

Every political movement needs its role models. Revolutions are no different. Role models need to have credibility. As role model, a lead revolutionary sets a personal example as to what it means to be a revolutionary in their particular cause. A leader may demonstrate this by (1) performing some of the duties required of non-leadership co-revolutionaries OR (2) have a history of having already done some of those tasks. Being a role model in the context of a revolution can be about establishing credibility, fear, love or respect for the leadership.

A lead revolutionary will likely gain greater support by demonstrating that the sacrifices to be made for the revolution will be shared by all involved but not necessarily equally. For obvious reasons, it may not be prudent for a leader to be on the front lines in an armed struggle or physical altercation with the status quo. However, it might just be precisely what needs to happen. It's up to the leader to determine the extent to which it's necessary to go to be a role model for supporters of a revolution.

Leaders can demonstrate commitment with the front line fighters by highlighting how many attempts to assassinate them have been made or how many death threats they have received. These events may already be public knowledge. In any case, it assures the front line combatants that their leader is also risking life and limb, despite these dangers, for the cause. The same can be said for less dangerous methods like calling for a boycott, a march or seeking financial commitments. The important point is that leaders must show some amount of risk that cements the trust and commitment of co-revolutionaries.

ORGANIZER

Excellent organization is a key component to the successful execution of a revolution. It would not be overstating the matter by saying that few political acts require the level of organization that a revolution requires. A revolutionary acting in an organizer's role must possess the skills to manage various, and sometimes conflicting, interests and personalities of people involved. Often, organizers in a revolution receive little to no publicity. They don't receive the praise and honors that a leader may receive. However, no matter how charismatic, persuasive or committed a leader is to the cause, it will absolutely fail without skilled organizers.

Organizers may be tasked with creating ways for information to be communicated, where meetings are to be held, as well as mobilizing people and support for needs of the cause. For example, there may be a need for some co-revolutionaries to remain nomadic so as not to be easily targeted by the status quo. So, an organizer might be charged with securing places to shelter the nomadic members of the cause. This may also include providing the routes to be taken and recommending the best times to move. Organizers also may be charged with the same tasks as it relates to the storage and movement of resources or supplies like food or weapons.

Though an organizer's role in a revolution may be less "high profile" than that of a leader or combatant, their involvement is a consideration in every step of the planning process. Organizers risk being punished, killed, imprisoned or financially ruined like any other revolutionary involved in the cause. An organizer can sometimes be privy to highly sensitive and confidential information. Depending upon the level of access an organizer has to the internal workings of the revolution, or the leadership, they can be used to dismantle the entire revolutionary enterprise if they decide to defect. This can make them primary targets for capture or for interrogation by the opposition as they are generally more easily accessible and believed to be more vulnerable than other members of the revolution.

TRAINER

A revolutionary as trainer is responsible for imparting skills to co-revolutionaries. This can be a difficult role as training must often be conducted in complete secrecy. This is particularly true where such training may involve fighting, combat or military related training. The trainer may be required to effectively train people at odd hours or in remote and hidden locations. In addition to time and location challenges, trainers may also have to conduct new or additional training as the revolution is unfolding. If they are not effective at doing this it could mean unnecessary delays, and in some cases, outright cessation of the revolution.

Lack of necessary resources to deliver the training can add another level of difficulty for trainers. Unlike a typical enterprise or organization, a revolution tends to deplete its resources at a much quicker rate. Executing a revolution is like running up hill rather than down hill. Until a revolution establishes enough momentum it will always be an up hill battle. Regardless of the abundance or lack of resources, the revolutionary serving in a trainer role must find a way to effectively deliver said training. Given the stakes involved in a classical revolution (i.e. overthrow of the government or political system) these trainers possess a motivation likely unmatched in any other political act.

Trainers in a revolution can deliver training in several areas. The type and extent of the training will be dictated by the specific goals set by the leadership. Some types of training administered include weapons, technological, language, ideological and doctrinal beliefs as well as intelligence gathering. Training may also include understanding laws and specific legal rights. Lastly, co-revolutionaries may be trained on how to respond if they are threatened, incarcerated, interrogated or their positions are otherwise compromised.

MOLE

In addition to fervor and commitment to the cause, a revolution needs a steady flow of information. This information needs to be accurate and timely. Information regarding the plans, communications, intentions and strategic direction of the status quo heavily influence the direction and execution of a revolution. Obtaining this information is one of the most dangerous tasks that can be asked of a revolutionary, therefore this role requires someone who is exceptionally committed and courageous.

Unless a mole is absolutely committed to the revolution, he or she can be one of the greatest weaknesses in a cause. As they often have access to both sides of the conflict, the temptation to act for personal gain, rather than in furtherance of the revolution, can be great. This sensitivity also makes the recruitment and vetting process for moles or "spies" more complex and problematic than for most other co-revolutionary roles.

SUPPLIER

Without sufficient resources a revolution is nothing more than an idea. Generally speaking, the word resources in this context means all of the materials, knowledge, personnel and finances needed to carry out a revolution. Planning the overthrow of a government or political system, no matter its size, requires substantial resources. Depending on the method and strategy of a particular revolution, the amount and type of resources required will vary considerably.

A revolution can benefit from many types of resources. These can include high level political or business connections, access to weapons in the case of violent overthrows, to basic essentials like food and water. Suppliers may provide free services such as legal defense, advice or facilities in the form of land, buildings or their personal residences. In violent revolutions, a nurse or physician might provide free first aid and medical services to co-revolutionaries injured during combat or other physical engagements with the status quo. A revolutionary as supplier serves as fuel for the cause.

COMBATANT

The revolutionary as combatant is likely the first image that comes to mind when one thinks of a revolutionary. The image of a classical revolutionary is of a person dressed in military-like garb, armed and leading co-revolutionaries into bloody shoot outs against the status quo. Alternatively, the image of angry individuals storming government buildings, burning people's homes and participating in similar types of public violence against the status quo. Kidnapping people or threatening to kill hostages is another thought that may come to mind when thinking of the revolutionary as combatant. Many people also likely think of men rather than women when it comes to revolutionary combatants. This is not always accurate as women also engage in combat.

It seems nearly impossible to think about a revolution without simultaneously thinking of a combatant. Today, many are unable to distinguish a revolutionary combatant from a terrorist. Unfortunately, due to the violent nature of classical revolutions (e.g. the overthrow of a government or its political system) anyone fighting in a revolution can be labeled a terrorist. This label is mostly used by the status quo or any person who opposes the revolution. Revolutionary activity becomes even more difficult to discern when combatants' understanding of nation management is inextricably tied to their religious beliefs. With this thorough understanding of the classical revolutionary model, we now move on to Neo-Revolutionary activity.

PROTOTYPE FOR NEO-REVOLUTIONARY ACTIVITY

> The people are in truth the only legitimate proprietors of the soil and government.
>
> ~Thomas Jefferson, Revolutionary & Third President of The United States of America

When a belief about something has been held in the public's collective consciousness for an extended period of time, it may seem impossible to change that belief. To do so, can invite ridicule, doubt, scorn and misunderstanding. This is particularly so regarding deeply held religious or political beliefs. That notwithstanding, when humankind is beckoned by nature's call to evolve, someone must be willing to take the first step onto that path. He or she must carve out the initial pathway into the unknown with assurance that the impulse which led to this new precipice will be sufficient to sustain the effort. Inspired by the American tradition of revolution, I now attempt to redefine the role of a revolutionary in contemporary American society.

It is tempting to simply relate events of the American Revolution and thereafter conclude that we ought to do as the founder's of this country did. Simply remembering the speeches, men and women, battles and events of the American Revolution, while perhaps evoking nostalgia, will not suffice for our present endeavor. No, in this particular case looking back will only result in focusing on the events of a foggy distant past and satisfaction with that feeling. We must resist. Those Americans were people of their day as we must be of ours. They met the challenge of their day (throwing off the shackles of unjust foreign rule) driven by a revolutionary spirit unprecedented in western culture at that time.

All that we may salvage from that past is the American revolutionary spirit itself. Scores of books, monuments, statues, paintings and memorials have already preserved their efforts. Presently, we must move beyond mere admiration and become ourselves those that inspire today's Americans. We must inspire the men, women and children of our families, our neighborhoods, our cities and our states. We need not concern ourselves even with future American generations yet unborn. Our precious responsibility is to resurrect and preserve the American revolutionary spirit upon which this nation was built.

If I must make any further reference to the revolutionary spirit of the past I will do so only in this way. First, I believe that Americans of the first revolutionary period took the responsibility of nation building and management far more seriously than Americans do today. That is not to say that Americans today are not deeply concerned or don't care about the condition of this nation. Rather, I say that they have thrown up that responsibility to politicians and the government. Their preoccupation with meaningless entertainment, gossip and quarrels of the day has allowed that quintessential revolutionary spirit of the American people to be completely overshadowed.

Americans today have been lulled into cocoons of complacency, ignorance, divisiveness and fear. Political action has devolved into endless fights between Democrats and Republicans. Americans have made each other the enemy. They carry out these manufactured differences for the government and politicians who are manipulating each of their thoughts and actions like puppets on a string. Forget about conspiracies and other such nonsense. Americans have freely given up that which their predecessors valued and cherished.

They are content to be engrossed in their petty differences erected along color lines, sexual orientation and similar issues.

They are too willing to attack fellow Americans but become cowards in response to government abuses. Content with flying the American flag, lighting firecrackers and singing the National Anthem with hand over heart, their meekness dishonors those revolutionaries who came before them. How many Americans have actually read the Bill of Rights? More importantly, how many Americans know why it was crafted and adopted? Was it to ensure the right to kill other Americans? To become a mere talking piece or bone of contention between political parties?

The American revolutionary spirit of old would scare most Americans today. I imagine that the impotence of today's revolutionary spirit would cause the government to label revolutionaries such as George Washington, Thomas Jefferson and Benjamin Franklin as terrorists if they walked among us. Likewise, what do you think those revolutionaries would think of today's Americans? Would they even think they are Americans? Would they applaud the low level of public political discourse, lack of in depth knowledge of what the government does, how it makes its laws and enforces them? How it abuses its authority?

The irrefutable fact is that America is a nation that was founded upon a revolutionary spirit. I will not recount the language used by so many of those well documented voices. But, how did American revolutionaries achieve the liberties and freedom which today so many Americans admire and exercise? They had to fight some bloody battles. That's what they determined was necessary to assert their rights and independence from the government to which they were subject. They believed that government of the people by the people was the natural order of things.

Their revolutionary spirit led them to a profound understanding which most Americans today would be afraid to think let alone publicly assert. In a democracy, government ought to have a respectful fear of the people not vice versa. That governing others is a privilege and not a right. We must ever be on guard against abuses by the government. Alexander Hamilton wrote in the Federalist Papers: "History will teach us…those men who have overturned the liberties of republics the greatest number have begun their career, by paying an obsequious court to the people, commencing Demagogues and ending Tyrants." Their American revolutionary spirit led them to complete dismissal of their government and its political system. Their revolution was an example of the classical variety. Valiant, yet protracted and bloody.

Today, I propose Americans who really care about the present conditions of this country revive the revolutionary spirit which produced it. The revolutionary spirit that Americans have inherited but lost must be reborn and made new. There are two major paradigm shifts that will be necessary to invoke and maintain the revolutionary spirit needed in our day. First, the previous expression of the American revolutionary spirit should not be copied or applied today. It should be non-violent.

Secondly, we must radically redefine revolution itself to meet our present day conditions. Overthrowing the government need not be the goal. It's unnecessary. Rather, we need to ensure absolute transparency of government activity via firsthand and unfiltered means. This is the natural evolutionary step in revolutionary thought and action in this democracy.

A NON-VIOLENT REVOLUTION

A non-violent revolution sounds like a contradiction. As stated previously, until now, the definition and meaning of revolution was the violent or forcible overthrow of a government or existing political system. The American Revolution, like all others in history, was one punctuated by violence. Today, we must adopt a new definition and understanding of revolution which will also aid us in understanding Neo-revolutionary activity. In the first chapter of this book, we stated the five components of legitimate revolutionary activity. We now define revolution and add a sixth and final component to that understanding.

Here-forward, revolution shall be defined as the attempt, by a citizen, to secure direct and unfiltered transparency of government action through any means non-violent. In crafting this definition, great care was taken to balance several interests and concerns. First, it needed to maintain the radical intensity of the classical definition. Second, it needed to leave room for multiple interpretations and expressions by revolutionaries. Third, it needed to establish a higher moral ground for engagement in revolutionary activity. Lastly, it needed to be restricted to individuals with the exclusive right to exercise it.

Let us exam this new definition of revolution in greater detail. This definition has four distinct clauses. They are the following:

I. **The attempt by a citizen**

II. **to secure direct and unfiltered transparency**

III. **of government action**

IV. **through any means non-violent**

CLAUSE I: The attempt by a citizen…

Revolutions are one of the most volatile yet valiant political acts that may be performed. This new definition does not diminish its seriousness, nor was it intended to do so. However, it was meant, in part, to limit who has the right to engage in revolutionary political activity. Clause I strictly limits this to citizens of the state. This means that though a revolution may have an impact globally, it ought to be exclusively a national effort.

Any foreign person, entity or government ought not aid or incite a revolution in another country. This is a tall order given the global interdependence of nations today. It is the responsibility of each nation's citizen's to erect, define or execute a revolution. Revolution is domestic business. Insisting that they be sparked and executed by citizens alone ensures that the parties involved are not unduly influenced or directed by foreign interests who may have other issues, legitimate or not, with the country experiencing a revolution.

Any non-citizen or foreign support solicited to assist in a revolution disqualifies and delegitimizes the act as a revolution, but not necessarily as a political act. However, should verified information be made public by a non-citizen, or foreign source, which may prove useful to the revolutionaries they may naturally elect to to take into consideration said information as it has become part of the public domain. This information should not be exclusively relied upon to act against the state or engage in revolutionary activity without a preponderance of proof that it is indeed legitimate. Otherwise, it would violate clause number two which we will now discuss.

CLAUSE II: …to secure direct and unfiltered transparency

One of the greatest barriers to trusting governments, is the the lack of transparency. Many citizens in America, regardless of party affiliation, don't believe they are getting the full facts when the government communicates with them. When major events occur they are often fed prescripted responses by government officials. Their benign, and often meaningless, updates do little to directly address or assuage the concerns of the people.

The governments perfunctory updates result in greater suspicion, cynicism or detachment by many citizens. These sentiments, compounded over extended periods of time within the collective consciousness of Americans, has resulted in problems such as low voter turnout and disinterest in civic engagement. The level of corruption and abuse by many politicians has inflated to such epic proportions that it seems the best (and only) way to verify government action is through direct first hand knowledge of the facts.

Direct and unfiltered transparency would require citizen access to materials and resources generally unavailable or restricted to the general public. They may also likely be highly confidential. Materials may include any and all non-public resources used by, or issued to, a government employee or official. If it suspected that a government official has used his or her position for personal gain or to harm citizens, and such behavior is verified, then citizens must decide whether to make this fact public knowledge.

This clause also addresses the increasingly weak and partisan investigative journalism we see today. News sources, both print and media, have collapsed into mere instruments of spin and marketing billboards for large corporations. They have become more interested in ratings, mind numbing gossip and tangents and are generally of no use in keeping the government honest. Direct and unfiltered transparency will remove their unnecessary sensationalism and distractions. Perhaps it may also encourage some of them to return to their roots of truly investigating events and not merely reporting hearsay or "the facts."

CLAUSE III: …of government action

Government action includes any and all activity for which a government employee, agent or appointed/elected official engages that is related to the responsibilities for which he/she has been employed or elected. Additionally, this definition extends to the improper or illegal use and exercise of their position (or resources allocated to them) for private gain. If their activity is suspected to have been conducted in order to withhold, divert or hide information that could harm or has harmed the public, citizens may decide if it ought to be revealed to the public.

CLAUSE IV: …through any means non-violent (the 6th component)

Revolution is a political act. Under the new paradigm, a revolution must be nonviolent. All human endeavors are subject to potential error. We are a mixture of complex emotional, spiritual and psychological elements. Too many are easily stirred to anger and violence. Their passions drive them to and fro, from one extreme to another, in the course of a single day. The mere thought of committing a violent act requires, in part at least, for us to call on a less desirable (though natural) human quality we possess.

It's natural for one to respond violently to another when being directly attacked. There is a deep primal instinct to live. Its energy is stronger in some than others. No matter the strength or weakness of this energy in people, they will always feel justified in defending themselves if violently attacked. In many violent situations, being directly attacked does not give one opportunity to think, only to react. The laws in America are not unique in recognizing this natural instinct and therefore has written protections into its penal codes providing exculpatory grounds for violence committed in self-defense under particular circumstances.

Violence committed in a revolution is of a completely different sort. When the violent overthrow of a government or political system (classical revolution) is contemplated, one must construct a sentiment equivalent to or greater than the feeling of being physically attacked. This means that there may be a period of pre-reflection of days, months or years before deciding to act. The period of reflection is of secondary concern as to what ultimately is to be decided…to hurt people or not. The decision to initiate violence of any sort almost always puts innocent people in harm's way. This is especially true in classical (i.e. violent) revolutions.

The decision to proactively utilize violence to solve or address political conflicts only occasionally ends in a better situation. Unfortunately, the history of humanity is still taught in no small part through wars and violence. Depending on who's telling the story, the people who participated in the conflict will be classified as *good* or *bad*. These horrifically bloody wars, revolutions and counter-revolutions can be said to have resulted in only one consistent outcome, the death of many people. This violence, utterly gratuitous at times, has been valorized in song, writing and art throughout the ages. Some even believed their actions to be sanctioned by God.

These various attempts to remember and honor those who have fallen in battle are themselves today simultaneously the symbols of much pain, heartache, anger and conflicts. For example, in America, indigenous Americans have had to endure the glamorization of the utter decimation of their culture, land and ways of life. There are stories, monuments, statues, movies and other nostalgic memorabilia across the country that remind them every day of their loss. Yet for another segment of the population these are all reminders of victory and a source of pride. The humanity of each party to violent acts, whether the deliverer, recipient or witness, is diminished with each occurrence.

Property may be repaired and damaged reputations may be restored. But, as life is even more valuable than these, we must be willing and able to achieve revolutionary ends through means nonviolent. Today's revolutionary must adopt this higher ethical ground in order to preserve life. Should they have acted in error they may rest assured that their error did not include intentional death of others. That said, it is highly unlikely that the status quo (government) will hold itself to such a high standard. It may seek to hurt or kill revolutionaries wherever they may be found. The Neo-revolutionary who is truly committed to justice, rather than some lesser motive, must weigh whether he or she is prepared to be a revolutionary of our time.

To balance out the nonviolence requirement, freer reign will likely need to be given to revolutionaries to exercise any and all other nonviolent means in furtherance of the revolution. What those means are will depend on the ethics and moral compass of the day. If reason prevails, the means selected will be commensurate with the perceived or actual harm of government actions.

One may ask whether "through any means nonviolent" may include breaking laws. We've already discussed the de facto illegal nature of revolutionary acts. So, obviously the answer is yes. Many may feel such license to break laws will result in chaos or anarchy. Nothing could be further from the truth. If it were so, we would already be in a state of anarchy. To understand this issue more completely, some time must be spent reflecting on laws and their validity. We'll limit our example specifically to America as this book is directed to its specific context and circumstances.

In America, there is a well defined process for making laws. An idea for a law (called a bill) is presented to a Representative by another Representative or citizen. A Representative is a member of Congress. There are 435 members in the U.S. House of Representatives which are divided among the 50 states. The number of representatives a state has is based on its number of people. Representatives are elected every two years.

A Representative must garner support from other Representatives about the bill and secure a sponsor. Once a spon-

sor is secured, the bill is then introduced to the House of
Representatives. The bill will undergo review, analysis and
revisions. If the bill is successful (i.e. receives a majority of
yes votes), it goes up to the U.S. Senate for additional exam-
ination and similar debates conducted in the House of Representatives. There are 100 Senators. The House of Representatives coupled with the Senate are collectively called the
Congress. (total of 535 members)

If the bill receives a majority of the Senate's votes, it is
sent to the President to be signed. The President may respond by (1) signing the bill at which point it becomes law;
(2) veto or refuse to sign the bill and send it back to Congress. If after further review of the bill, Congress reaffirms it
with 2/3 support it will become law; (3) do nothing (pocket
veto) and if Congress is in session the bill becomes law au-
tomatically after 10 days. If Congress is not in session the
bill does not become a law.

The creation and passing of laws is quite an elaborate
process. Given the level of scrutiny and competing interests
involved in the process, it is extraordinary that any laws get
passed. In the minds of many, once a law has been passed it
is binding and valid upon citizens. As the government has
gone through the proper procedure to make the law, there
ought naught be any further questioning of its legitimacy. If
citizens were allowed to ignore laws, society would be un-
manageable. We would lose any sense of social cohesion. I
don't entirely agree with this view nor does the history of
this nation.

What I have just described is merely a legislative process.
While a process to makes laws may be more or less efficient
or prudent, that does not make the law just or binding. The
American citizen who knows the history of the revolutionary
spirit in this country will not agree that a law being passed,
in and of itself, makes it binding or just. In 1773, the British
Parliament passed the Tea Act of 1773. It needed to offload a

large surplus of extra tea. This surplus was being held in warehouses in London and was a serious financial burden to the British East India Company. Additionally, Great Britain did not like that tea was being illegally smuggled into its colonies which included America. The goal was essentially to create a right to impose taxes unilaterally for tea exports but not pay tax for imported tea from the colonies.

America had no representatives in the British Parliament. As a colony ruled by the Crown, America enjoyed only semi-autonomous freedom to act. The Tea Act of 1773 received the blessing of the Crown on May 10, 1773. Given the subordinate position of America, it would seem natural that they would obey the provision of the Act as it had other laws and legislation. Much to the chagrin of Great Britain, American revolutionaries had a different opinion about this Act. A meeting in Boston was held to decide on how to respond to this abuse of authority.

In protest, on December 16, 1773, several revolutionaries boarded a British East India Company ship that was loaded with tea and parked in the Boston Harbor. Once aboard the ship, the men began dumping the chests of tea into the harbor. This became known as the Boston Tea Party. Great Britain responded with the Coercion Acts (a.k.a. Intolerable Acts) in 1774. Among the provisions of these Acts was that Boston's self-governing allowances were abolished. Furthermore, Boston's commerce activity was to cease. A year later, in 1775, after attempts at petitioning Great Britain to repeal the Acts, the American Revolution began.

In America, assuming a law has been legally passed only makes it fifty percent legitimate. Citizens' consent to adhere to that law provides the other half of legitimacy. Therefore, breaking laws in furtherance of the aims of legitimate revolutionary activity should not even be called civil disobedience or unrest, but a duty and right of every American citizen. It is incumbent upon every person of this nation to be willing to take any steps, short of violence, to ensure that the laws imposed on them are valid, binding and just.

Conversely, the legitimacy of a revolution is to be determined by the citizens seeking to engage in such activity. It is not a proposition to be put forward and debated by the government. Many may fear that by *any means non-violent* gives too much license for people to act. They'll say that this freedom is too broad and society will collapse into chaos. They may warn us that the social contract will become meaningless. On the contrary, nothing jeopardizes the stability of a nation in the same way that unjust laws and government corruption does.

Most risks, but certainly not all, that may arise while acting in furtherance of a revolution must be absorbed in order to remedy or preclude the greater harm of corrupt or dishonest government action. The government is charged with the supreme responsibility of managing the political health of the nation. When it has become parasitic on the body of the nation it must be exposed and corrected by citizens. One potent way to combat the toxic and colossal breakdown of confidence in government caused by corrupt action is some sort of Neo-revolution activity.

Citizens who participate in the Neo-revolution must no longer see corrupt governments as adversaries needing to be destroyed. Neo-revolutionaries must adopt a more mature vision of their relationship with government. Rather than acting as dynamite they need to act as microscope. Not as police officers but as physicians. Americans need to move towards a new understanding of management of the government by the citizens. Americans can no longer be reactive but must become proactively involved in the affairs of government.

Revolution, as presently defined, must be a dynamic activity. Citizens must effectively cease to see themselves as spectators but instead more like the fourth branch of government…a kind of Citizens Bureau of Government Transparency. Revolution is not an enterprise for the feint of heart. It may cause serious social upheaval. The risk of personal harm will likely be great. Fortunately, for the status quo (i.e. government), fear will deter the vast majority of citizens from thinking about revolution let alone participating in one. Though many citizens may believe government corruption is wrong, they may still lack the courage to meet the standard set by the the founding revolutionaries of America and do anything about that abuse or corruption.

Most Americans, including myself, do not want to see this country suffer unnecessarily. Not as the result of nefarious government action nor as a result of their personal behavior in their official capacity. This sentiment will tend to temper the call for revolutionary activity. Every revolution will require some level of cooperation from other citizens. The heated debate between supporters and detractors regarding a revolution will greatly impact whether it actually materializes. Many may not trust every day Americans to debate and make such serious decisions. I have the utmost faith in conscious and informed Americans to evaluate the efficacy of any revolutionary activity.

Let nothing that has been written so far be wrongly interpreted as encouragement to break the laws indiscriminately. The point is, that breaking a particular law ought not prevent the commencement of legitimate revolutionary activity. Cowards will employ every means, especially fear, to stifle revolution to address corrupt or dishonest government action. We must disregard such diversions for a greater cause. Revolutionary activity should never be an option where presently existing legitimate avenues to attain the same goal already exist. Given the strict requirements to justify a legitimate revolution, we now consider what might be at least one plausible tool for Neo-revolutionary activity.

TRANSPARENCY AS A RIGHT

Could the straggling thoughts of individuals be collected,
they would frequently form materials for wise and able men
to improve into useful matter. (from Common Sense)

~Thomas Paine, Revolutionary, Author & English-American
Political Activist

The integration of technology into daily life and society has significantly challenged our understanding of what is means to be human. Many would argue that it has advanced past integration and into outright reliance or burdensome invasion of our lives. One can scarcely perform a single act, in private or public, without somehow that action being recorded, captured or stored. The public's acceptance of what is tantamount to unlimited surveillance has been achieved primarily through entertainment, legislation, media and government's trafficking in fear.

This paternalistic monitoring of citizens has morphed into pernicious and predatory abuse upon the part of the government. Its obsessive activity has resulted in unwarranted spying on wealthy chief executives of American corporations, world class athletes, famous artists, prominent leaders of faith communities, outspoken entertainers and you. Moreover, prying into private affairs of innocent citizens is done with even greater disregard because of citizen's inability to prevent this intrusive government action.

In our day, it is evident that government is unable to exercise consistent prudence, or reasonableness, with regard to privacy rights of innocent citizens. We are inundated with claims that all of this surveillance is for our own good. The government claims that there are too many bad people in the population which justifies their unfettered surveillance. Yet it detests the acts of those individuals, who may possess a more inclusive sense of justice, for revealing first hand proof of corrupt government action. We have seen the scorn with which those called "whistleblowers" are treated.

Dear reader, consider this. On any given day, certain government agencies or officials can have access to, and likely can describe with greater detail, your personal day-to-day activity better than your closest friends or family members. Each time you make a purchase involving an electronic fund transfer it is recorded. Don't think that by using cash only for purchases it will make you immune to surveillance because it won't. Almost any building or facility you enter has a number of video cameras recording everything you do. Not to mention public streets in America are increasingly becoming lined with cameras.

Most mobile devices used today are connected to some type of network. Whether that device is on or off often makes no difference in wether you can be tracked and monitored. Every electronic communication you send or receive will be permanently stored forever on a server. The government can force any such communications to be made available upon demand. Where companies, or any individuals collecting these communications, refuse to release these materials the government simply invokes other means to get the information. One of those tactics includes making a claim of a national security threat. They also may employ legislative influence and other means of coercion to force capitulation by companies or individuals.

The government has forced libraries and bookstores to reveal what books have been read or purchased by citizens. Phone calls are regularly recorded even where no threat to society is present or even suspected. Postal mail and letters and sensitive exchanges between friends and family are indiscriminately opened, read or simply "go missing." Access to your money in any institution can be denied or seized by the government without your prior knowledge. You may suddenly become subject to frequent *random* tax audits and similar government acts of agitation.

As Americans, we must take some of the responsibility for a government that has assumed a position of watchdog over its citizens. Under the spell and need to be constantly stimulated and entertained, we have allowed two lamentable problems to emerge. First, the gross enrichment of companies that will generally put profits before concern of the people and secondly the creation of a nearly undetectable means of intrusion by the government.

When government is cloaked in the garb of your favorite brand, service or product, you may not realize that you are freely creating openings into aspects of your life to the government that they might not otherwise have had. I am not one who subscribes to conspiracy theories about the government. Nor has anything I have written so far intended to infer that any collusion between corporations and government exist. Whether such conspiracies or collusion actually exists is of no consequence. What matters is that the abusive government action of unwarranted invasions of privacy and paternalistic monitoring of citizens is pervasive.

The reality is that the near constant surveillance by the government has become a fact of life in America. If the government had the ethical or moral fortitude to self correct its own abusive action, and also limit citizen surveillance to legitimate cases, that would be digestible. We allegedly live in a democracy. However, dictators, despots and totalitarian regimes outshine our government when it comes to honesty and truth. Under those forms of government, citizens are given no illusion of fairness and equality before the law.

Their liberties, freedom or privacy (to the extent that they possess any) are subject to the idiosyncratic whims of the state or leader.

Our government insults our intelligence and our loyalty. It points a shameful finger at other countries decrying their corruption, backwardness and brutishness. It tells us we ought to be thankful that "you don't live in a country like that." It says we are the freest and greatest country the world has ever seen. It teaches you that "American Exceptionalism" has produced a country that is the envy of the world. This meaningless filibustering always ends with the trite cliche "God bless America." It's all hollow sophistry. A hypocrite has no greater standing in the eyes of the Almighty than a tyrant. Hypocrisy is the twin brother of tyranny.

No government will ever be infallible for one simple reason. They are comprised of people. People are flawed. That said, some put a premium on justice more than others. So long as this remains the case, citizens must always be on guard against government abuse. The number of instances of government abuse has grown too many in number to list. Yet, our government would have its citizens believe that it nonetheless is still entitled to our complete trust and faith to act in our best interest. I disagree. We simply cannot allow this facade to continue any longer. Their belief, expressed through their abusive action, in the right to illegal and unquestioned surveillance and hacking of citizens without any credible justification must be addressed.

We also should no longer accept, without transparency, that men and women of this nation are being sent into wars abroad to protect America's interests rather than for less honorable reasons. We cannot accept that political campaigns are being conducted with more integrity than not. We must refuse to accept being forced to vote for candidates who are unworthy of public trust or who have acted in unethical ways unbecoming of a government employee or official. Government must be made to understand that the trust they have been given to manage the affairs of Americans is not a right, but a responsibility and privilege.

The answer cannot be that sufficient procedures and laws are already in place to mitigate abusive government action. Apparently, this is not so. If it were, we would not be experiencing the level of deceit and deception displayed by our government. A wolf will never condemn another wolf for slaughtering hens in a hen house. Likewise, a government official wrapped in various legal protections not enjoyed by regular citizens, will rarely condemn the corrupt actions of a colleague save the possibility that there might be some personal or political incentive for doing so.

Sometimes poison can produce its own cure. The government's abuse of our privacy, and utter disregard of our trust, may have unwittingly provided the spark for a legitimate Neo-revolutionary response. The government has only one incentive in continuing its illegal behavior. That being we have put it into position to abuse citizen rights without any concern of corrective action. Its autonomy, and lack of citizen management, has led to it acting with utter disregard for rights. Government wrongly concludes that it is justified in monitoring innocent citizens but citizens are not justified in monitoring and correcting its illegal or unethical activity.

Throughout history, corruption and dishonesty have shown their presence even among members of the clergy. This was the case despite believing they were being watched by an omnipotent God. Is it any surprise, where no such God need even be considered by a secular state, that our government acts with even greater impunity? It is not within our capacity to rid the human race of fallibility. However, as it regards those whom we allow to govern us, we can take direct action to curtail and minimize their abuse of our trust domestically and abroad.

As a nation expands and becomes as ethnically diverse as America, it is only natural that schisms among its citizens will arise. Even in a culturally homogenous nation, differences arise though perhaps not for all the same reasons they do in a more diversely populated country. Given this dynamic, and its ability to divide and distract citizens from important concerns, we must seek and seize every opportunity to act in harmony with one another. Revolution, as now defined, provides a means for citizens to unite for a common good regardless of ethnicity, creed or political orientation.

You may disagree with another citizen's religion, politics or their food preferences. But, all can agree that abusive government action is an assault on the nation. America is an infant in terms of its length of existence. It is not even 300 years old as of this writing. There are other nations which have several thousand years of history. Any suggestion that the founders of America have answered and addressed every question for all time is to express unforgivable ignorance. America, despite claims to the contrary by some, can not call itself the greatest civilization of all…yet. This nation has not yet been perfected and there is much work to be done. Nothing will prevent that progress more than abusive government action and lack of transparency.

For over two hundred years the importance of the right to vote has been hailed as one of the ultimate rights of a citizen in a democratic society. While this right is extremely valuable, today it is less valuable than transparency of government action. The right to vote was created for two primary reasons. First, to allow citizens a participatory role in the management of public affairs that could impact them. Secondly, that those elected to public office felt some real accountability to voters who place them into office. In theory, this all sounds plausible. In practice, it has left much to be desired.

The right to vote has not been able to significantly or consistently create a true sense of accountability to citizens. Americans have been lulled into believing that they live in the greatest country in part because they have a right to vote. Unfortunately, the mere right to vote has no substantial ability to hold government officials accountable for improper action. Documents can be classified or sealed for 30 or 40 years! That is literally several decades after wrong acts have been committed. This leaves us (as citizens) with decades to deal with the extended damage and aftermath long after those who have committed the acts have left office, grown old and feeble or died.

Consider this. What would life be like today if Americans had obtained access to a false accusation that led to the Vietnam War? How many thousands of families (not just American) might have had a longer life with their son, brother, mother, wife, husband or daughter? How many homeless veterans on the streets of America might not be there? How many veterans would not be suffering from mental illnesses, health problems or have had to have limbs amputated or be unemployed? Disagreement about that war tore America apart and the wounds still exist. The same could be said about invading Iraq under the false pretext that it possessed weapons of mass destruction. The grief and destruction that these events caused are not likely to go away. Perhaps transparency could have prevented all of this and so much more.

Imagine what the past 60 years in America could have been like had these and other unnecessary conflicts been averted because of transparency. War is undoubtedly lucrative for those who profit in human carnage. Citizens armed with transparency can have much more impact on government action than those merely possessing a right to vote. The global nature of world politics, coupled with the interdependence of economic and natural resources, demands that American citizens take a more active role in knowing what the government intends to do and not simply what it has done. The actions of our government has great impact on the lives of others. We must take this responsibility very seriously.

Heretofore, we've spoken only of the global implications and value of what greater transparency of government action could produce. Lest the reader think that the positive domestic impact of such transparency would be any less, we shall dispel any such thought. The domestic impact of transparency would be felt more fully and immediately at home. Likewise, as citizens the ability to meaningfully address government abuse or bad action will be greater. Shared soil, common language and cultural familiarity all make for more expedient detection, exposure and resolution of improper government action.

Under the Neo-revolution paradigm, the present role of the American citizen in politics as pony or pawn is eliminated. Classical revolutions have had a clearly definable path due in part to their primary goal and main method of expression. (i.e. force and violence) The spirit of revolution is a creative one. Its expression will be determined by the collective consciousness of the American citizens of the day. Whatever form or expression it takes, let it be reasonable yet allow for spontaneity. One group of citizens among us may prove to be extremely helpful in Neo-revolutionary activity today…hackers. Let us now take a brief look behind the curtain of mystery that is the world of the hacker.

ENTER THE HACKER

Every nation has a particular character, in which it differs from all others that have been, that are, and possibly from all that are to come; for it does not appear that the Divine Father of nations ever repeats himself and creates either two nations or two men exactly alike.

~Theodore Parker, American Transcendentalist, Pastor, Reformer

Hackers are defined not by nationality, gender or political beliefs. They are defined by what kind of hacking they do and for what purposes. Hackers are not limited by geography as their activities are nearly exclusively carried out electronically, through computers and computer networks. Few words today evoke a combination of fear, misunderstanding, anger and curiosity than *hacker*. Most often we imagine any number of sinister images of individuals hiding in cyberspace seeking to prey upon innocent victims. This imagery is not entirely unwarranted.

The context in which this word is mentioned is almost always negative. It usually involves someone (or a group) illegally accessing and penetrating security programs, databases, files or networks. Banks, credit card companies, social media sites, corporations and schools are among the common targets. Hackers then take the information and attempt to sell or exchange it for nefarious and malicious purposes. Government and military agencies must defend against perpetual efforts at hacking their information. However governments, including the US, are routinely engaged in hacking into files and systems of foreign governments ostensibly in the interest of national security.

Hacking is an act deemed *good* or *bad* depending on who's doing the hacking, what was hacked and for what purpose it was done. The reality is that anyone (or entity) that uses a computer, cell phone, the internet or electronic devices is susceptible to being hacked. It's highly likely that you've already been hacked and don't realize it. The myth that our government is not surveilling and arbitrarily hacking citizen information has been debunked in our day. Whistle-blowers and others have revealed not only that this activity is happening but indiscriminately.

Some definitions of hacker include: (1) an expert at programming and solving problems with computers; and *(2) thinkers or people who enjoy exploring the details of programmable systems and how to stretch their capabilities. (*MIT Hacker Dictionary) Among some programmers, engineers and computer science professionals the word *hacker* is used simply to refer to another person like themselves. Additionally, Hackathons and HackFests are held in several technical hubs around the world including Silicon Valley. In these events the "hack" is short for explorative programming. They are not attended exclusively by engineers but also designers, developers, software experts and tech enthusiasts. Suffice to say, that while the layperson or non-technical enthusiast almost universally associates hacking or hackers with crime and illegal activity it is not so among the technical community.

THE THREE HATS

Hackers can generally be separated into one of three groups. One is called Black Hat Hacker. (here-forward BHH) BHH are the ones most people have heard about. They illegally hack into computers, files, systems, networks and computers of individuals or organizations.Their purpose is for personal gain, sabotage or other malicious reasons. The stolen information is often either sold or exchanged with a third party so that third party may use the information or data for malicious purposes.

The BHH was created in the hacker community to separate it from the general and widespread misconception of the meaning of hacker. In fact, within the hacker (i.e. programmer) community individuals or groups who use their technical skills for criminal and illegal purposes are called *crackers*. The unethical and illegal activity of a BHH is called cracking as in illegally breaking into a system, computer or network. Publicly the term hacker caught on and became synonymous with the criminal behavior done by BHHs.

Another group of hackers are called Gray Hat Hackers. (GHH) These hackers also illegally hack systems of other people and organizations. The main differences between a GHH and BHH is that a GHH doesn't hack for criminal purposes. Likewise, they may alert the hacked party of the security weaknesses, but only after they have executed the breach. Alternatively, if a GHH does not directly notify the hacked party of the breach it may simply make the breach known to the public. Nonetheless, the activities of an GHH can result in serious problems.

A third group of hackers is called White Hat Hacker. (WHH) These hackers are the polar opposite of BHHs. WHH hack systems for the purpose of protecting or fixing them. Any vulnerabilities discovered are then made known to the system owner. Furthermore, unlike a BHH or GHH, the WHH seeks permission to hack a system before attempting to hack into it. Additionally, a WHH does not disclose security breaches to third parties, attempt to sell information or otherwise profit in any criminal or malicious way from their activity.

Governments, corporations and organizations also employ hackers. Borrowing from a military strategy these hackers are assembled into independent groups called Red Teams. In America, these teams are assembled to proactively attack systems belonging to a government agency or private corporation to discover security vulnerabilities before anyone else does. The value of a Red Team is immeasurable. If they are effective at what they do it can save millions of dollars and perhaps just as many lives. It is in the spirit of Red Teams that a citizens' approach to transparency of government action may be approximately modeled with adjustments being made for the unique intricacies of such an endeavor.

Whatever one's feelings are about hackers or hacking, the reality is that it is part of contemporary life in America. The act itself may not be presently examined nor debated on legal grounds. Except under certain permissions granted to government by law, mutual consent in a legal contractual agreement, and very few other scenarios, it is prohibited. Yet, we find ourselves as citizens with our own government ignoring any restrictions or guidelines with regard to innocent citizens. As far as citizen hacking being illegal, there are many valid reasons why this should be so in a civil society. They are self-evident and need not be enumerated here.

I agree that a free license to hack the government on a mere whim would be imprudent. Unfortunately, as a practical matter, we are already there. Attempts to hack the government by people and foreign governments are a regular occurrence. But, the fact that our government and some people use a technique, tool or strategy to act criminally should not thereby disqualify citizens from discussing whether to use those same approaches for legitimate purposes. By analogy, mere ownership of a gun does not create a danger, but how it is used does. Hacking is the same. It can be used for illegal purposes or for legitimate purposes.

Hacking also need not be debated on moral grounds. That is, whether hacking is good or evil is not a question generally raised in a state which operates based exclusively upon civil law. Hacking would be perfectly acceptable to debate or analyze from a moral point of view if America was governed under religious or theistic laws. That said, given this debate and evaluation is to be carried out by citizens of America, many of which presumably have religious beliefs, they may decide that a moral argument for or against hacking the government for legitimate purposes has a place in the public debate.

Above all, this matter is a debate on ethical grounds. The debate should initially commence with whether hacking to ensure greater transparency of government action ought to be done. There is no question, or doubt, as to whether it can be done. It can. The "ought it be done" question is of primary importance because there is much to consider in terms of benefits versus risks. We've witnessed the downside of the government's zeal to build a nuclear bomb before giving enough consideration as to whether it *ought to be done*. Now we must live with the results of that decision for the foreseeable future.

As a practical matter, government will not be entirely excluded from the debates and discussions. They are citizens as well. They should be free to attend, and participate in, any public discussions but not act as a manager or authority figure in any way. Likewise, they should organize and hold public discussions as well if they desire to exercise greater control over the discussions. If the present state of government intrusion into citizen privacy is any indication of what its involvement in debates about this matter will be, then it will already be "present, watching and/or listening" in on such discussions without an invitation anyway.

These debates and discussions should be public. This transparency on the part of citizens raises the bar of how one ought to act in a civil society. It may perhaps also save citizens tax dollars that might be otherwise unnecessarily spent by government surveilling and hacking private discussions. Classrooms, campuses, libraries, coffee shops and parks can all serve as venues. Likewise, town hall meetings, neighborhood gatherings, dinner table chats and online exchanges should also take place. America is a such a vast country geographically speaking. It has many cultures and many different points of views. This discussion and debate has the possibility of not becoming mired in party or identity politics if it is open and focuses on the common interest at hand which is greater transparency of government action.

Governments are comprised of people. No person is infallible. Therefore, no government is infallible. In securing greater transparency of government action we need not, and simply can't, ensure perfection. But, we can reduce the unacceptable levels of privacy invasion protected under the US Constitution and laws of this land. We may also prevent the number and duration of unnecessary wars which send scores of Americans, and people of other nations, to the grave prematurely.

The government has the responsibility to act in the best interest of Americans. It has been given the power to do so. Government also has the greatest capacity to harm the nation and its citizens. Therefore, government needs to be held to a standard of transparency commensurate with these monumental responsibilities and privileges. Whether due to intentional disregard or less sinister reasons (such as the sheer size of the government machinery) the government is missing the mark when it comes to honoring the privacy rights of citizens and committing this country to unnecessary conflicts and wars.

Undoubtedly, there will be a number of government officials and employees who will object to any notion of transparency of the variety or scope being raised here for debate.

Like the Crown who once viewed the citizens of this nation as mere subjects of a colony, the government may hold a similar view about American citizens today. They will say that "you are too uninformed and untrained to meddle into such complex affairs." This merely being a caustic way of saying "you are too unsophisticated and ignorant to do anything but place a vote in a ballot box when summoned to do so." After which "your business with us has concluded."

Dear Americans, what shall be your response to this slander? Shall you be slapped on one cheek by insult and with disregard on the other? Or shall you be an American of your day as the founders were of theirs? You must find the courage to become more fully involved in the care of your country. Fortunately, unlike the revolutionary days of yore, today's proactive engagement need not be violent or bloody. While the government has the responsibility and privilege to act in citizens' best interest, more ethical and accurate execution of those duties needs to be secured. More laws or more government is not the answer. Nor is more voting. Presently, what the house needs is more windows. The task as American citizens is to decide where to place those windows.

BUGS & GLITCHES

When citizens engage in political action to hold their government accountable for their responsibilities, it can create a great deal of hostility. Collective political action becomes even more difficult when the population is as large and diverse as America. It is not uncommon for two citizens to be in total agreement about the desired end yet vehemently disagree about the proper means to achieve that end. Layer upon the logistical differences of opinion, culture, religious beliefs, gender and language barriers and the prospect of getting anything done together seems impossible.

Additionally, when a particular political act is not permitted by law, and there is no previous precedent for the type of act, that act will likely be met with even greater resistance by the government and perhaps skepticism by citizens. This particular political act of hacking the government raises many important concerns and questions. It takes little imagination to produce any number of doomsday scenarios should such an act be injudiciously executed. A single mistake, or irresponsible act on the part of a citizen engaged in revolutionary political acts could result in everything from valuable information being unnecessarily compromised to a threat to national security.

Aside from the many negative repercussions of this political act, there are myriad logistical, strategic and practical concerns that would warrant substantial analysis before deciding that this is a viable approach to address the two problems it aims to correct. Will hacking be preemptive, ongoing or random? Who will do the hacking and how will that be decided? Is there a selection process? Is a selection process even feasible or necessary? Under what guidelines and parameters ought citizens engage in this act? What is to be done with any information once accessed? These and so many other questions present themselves if the answer to the primary question of whether this ought to be done is "yes." That primary question has not been publicly debated yet.

The concern may also arise that if citizens decide to validate this as a political act that scores of unscrupulous citizens will decide to arbitrarily engage in hacking. That they will do so more for sport and play rather than based on valid political action or convictions. The parade of horribles connected to this type of political activity is real and should not be ignored or unduly considered. This government functions quite well in many areas. For now, the freedom we enjoy as Americans to speak or write with moderate censorship is considerable relative to most other countries.

As stated previously, the catalyst for considering hacking as a revolutionary act is to (1) correct the problem of government's unfettered surveillance and hacking of innocent citizens and (2) limit the number of perpetual wars and conflicts Americans are sent to fight under false or dubious pretenses. In the attempt to correct these two problems where the government is not meeting the mark, said attempts must not disrupt those areas where it is functioning satisfactorily.

For all of the legitimate concerns mentioned regarding engagement in this Neo-revolutionary activity, there are several counterbalancing factors that should significantly mitigate concerns. One such factor is fear. This fear is of two kinds. Many Americans are extremely afraid of the government. I would wager that this is true of the majority of Americans. They view government as an all powerful leviathan who can, and will, destroy them at will for any disobedience. The fear of being imprisoned, exiled, financially ruined or even killed will most assuredly prevent an overwhelming number of Americans from engaging in this kind of Neo-revolutionary activity. The second type of prohibitive fear would be the number of possible unintended or unforeseen negative consequences on the country that may result from hacking. It's the fear of the unknown.

Next, the lack of technical skills that presently exists amongst the American population is vast. Despite America's technological prowess, the percentage of Americans skilled on an expert level in programming, cybersecurity, network design and mathematics is minuscule compared to the total population of the country. Hacking on this level requires a certain specialized skill set that frankly most Americans have not taken the time to acquire. Nor is it likely that this type of political action will ignite a sudden interest in learning the highly technical skills hacking on this level requires. Even if some were so inclined, few would probably be willing to spend the requisite amount of time to learn enough to penetrate a network or system as well secured as one maintained by the government.

Additionally, political apathy is presently widespread in America. This apathy is presumably not restricted to non-technical professionals and non-engineers. At least some members of the technical profession likely share in this political apathy. So, even if a citizen is (1) not scared of the government (2) is willing to assume the potential negative outcomes of this type of political act as acceptable (3) possesses sufficient technical skills to engage in hacking at the highest levels of security, he or she would also have to have enough interest in matters of the State to act on those convictions in this particular way.

The type of American both capable and willing to engage in Neo-revolutionary acts of this nature would need to possess a high level of concern and interest in the affairs of this country. These convictions would need to be similar in intensity to those of the founders of this nation. Given the gravity at stake for both the actor and the country it's less likely that individuals would elect to frivolously engage in this type of activity. The repercussions for "getting it wrong" are such that anyone who began to take the steps to act would be immediately confronted with the seriousness of their actions. The founding revolutionary members of America knew this well. They decided it was worth it. What shall you decide?

Legitimate revolutionary acts often summon the best and brightest of a nation's citizens to execute them. The two abuses seeking to be corrected here are serious. The question of securing transparency through hacking as one possible solution, is now on the table. Time is not necessarily on the side of citizens in this debate. The longer it takes to implement a solution or corrective action the more government's abuse is likely to continue and compound. It's time to debate and decide the matter. Be bold yet prudent.

53

A house divided against itself cannot stand.

~Abraham Lincoln, American Statesman & Sixteenth President of The United States of America

Dear reader. This book could have easily filled four to five hundred pages. Its subject matter, political governance, has filled countless volumes of books and many library bookshelves. How to govern eventually becomes the question of the day in any civilized society which has elected preservation as a goal rather than lawlessness. It brings with it a long history much of which has been written in blood. Today, more bloodshed and violence cannot be our means to persuade or disagree with one another. The world is too interconnected for a nation like America to self destruct simply because it can't find nonviolent ways to manage itself. Our day calls for principled, rational and direct clashes of ideas.

This book has raised a bold question for debate among American citizens. The goal being to provide a solution to the two problems that have become parasitic on this nation and will eventually preclude its ability to continue to progress. One, the arbitrary and unrestricted surveillance and hacking of innocent citizens. Two, this country's initiation of, and participation in, wars and armed conflicts under dubious or false pretenses. Securing greater transparency of government action, as a matter of right, has been proposed as a topic for debate to significantly reduce these abuses.

As the government is unlikely to voluntarily give citizens meaningful and timely access to its activities, the question becomes how ought citizens secure greater transparency. More laws and procedures would simply lack any potency to force the government to comply or change its behavior. As the laws are made and passed by the government, citizens cannot naively believe that government will pass any laws that would tend to expose its abuses of power and of the public's trust.

Technology continues to impact government conduct, and politics generally, in unforeseen ways. The government has chosen to use this technology for not entirely noble or legal purposes. In regards to its citizens, it has chosen to intrude upon their personnel lives, thoughts and communications under the auspices of security. Its defense is that in order to maintain our safety in a dangerous world that they must arbitrarily surveil and hack innocent citizens. So government must violate everyone's rights and treat everyone like a criminal or terrorist in order to preserve public safety. Also, citizens should trust that government always acts in the public's best interest. This is reductio ad absurdum.

One wonders how listening to innocent intimate conversations between spouses and lovers or capturing email exchanges between grieving family members is in any way defensible by the government for any reason let alone security. The government might also add that anyone not involved in any criminal behavior should not have any concerns with the status quo. It is conceivable that a number of citizens would agree with this statement. But, that a small fraction of citizens might consent to being secretly surveilled and hacked cannot decide the matter. Moreover, it is highly likely that the moment that innocent data is used for ill purposes by the government against them they would resent having aloud such intrusions into their private lives.

It seems the government offers up the same argument in defense of perpetual war and violent conflicts. The argument is that there are a lot of bad people in the world that require policing or elimination. All the while never seeing itself as an instigator or catalyst of bad behavior. No, the government claims that every war it engages in is to protect American interests and never for unjust reasons. However, no specific verifiable information can be given to the public regarding why Americans are sent to die or kill others in these wars. Appeals to freedom, justice and other important concepts are launched at the American public by government. When those appeals cease to be effective they simply rely on fear. It always works. Then the media, which profits from public anxiety, constantly repeats and replays these statements to increase its ratings and collect ad money.

Not surprisingly, these wars or potential conflicts are promoted in nearly three exclusive situations. One, where there is an economic advantage to be had or valuable commodity involved. (e.g. oil) Two, where significant economic or technological growth occurs in a country viewed to be a threat to America. Third, where another country's soil can be exploited or strategically used as a theater of war to facilitate hostilities. Admittedly, there are individuals and nations who given the chance would like to conquer, destroy or otherwise injure America. America should reasonably and vigorously defend itself against any such attempts. However, indiscriminate war and violence should never be legitimized or normalized.

America is comfortably nestled thousands of miles away from the carnage of war. American citizens are often duped into supporting wars. To most Americans, except those being sent to fight, war is a television event. War happens *over there*. Against people that dress differently and who speak a foreign language. Americans go to work, entertain themselves and then leisurely check in on the war as they would their emails or text messages. Their homes are not blown up. Their children are not psychologically traumatized or physically mutilated. Their mothers and daughters are not raped and left for dead by foreign soldiers. They sit comfortably feeling that no planes will fly over to carpet bomb them. There is no experience of death or post war famine and disease.

The news is discouraged from showing coffins and body bags coming back to America. When an American plane goes down it's never because it was shot down but rather due to mechanical or pilot error. This bubble of illusion about the atrocities of war is created to sanitize the reality of it. Today, Americans are willing to endure wars because they've not really experienced its ravages. Only the families and friends of those veterans who come back maimed, permanently traumatized or in a coffin really experience war. But, come election time candidates running for office parade veterans across the stage to capture votes, not to truly honor these Americans. This after knowingly sending them into wars under unnecessary or fabricated pretenses. It's all so shameful. It can change. It must change.

However, when violent tentacles do reach America's soil, as it did on September 11, 2001, it becomes a national nightmare that may never be forgotten. Americans grieve, as they should, over the innocent loss of lives. Sadly, the government, through a thirst for war, has opened a pathway to more violence which has only increased the hatred of America. The government tells citizens that others hate America because of its way of life. They say people of other nations and cultures envy American freedom. Therefore, we must fight and kill them or else end up living as they do or under their rule. This is purely argumentum ad metum.

Again, the question for our consideration is not whether hacking can be used to significantly reduce these intentional abuses by our government. That it can be hacked is already established as evidenced by the breaches of security that have been made publicly known. There have likely been far more than the public may ever know. Our question is *ought* hacking be used by citizens to gain greater transparency of government action in order to minimize these two abuses and perhaps other presently unforeseen harms due to government action.

Hackers, or engineers, are not here being suggested as the only means to secure greater transparency. Rather, they could serve as a component of a potentially more comprehensive approach to holding the government to the standard which it is obliged to comply. Here is not the place to attempt a draft of what such a complete approach, or hacking in particular, would look like. Any such discussions are premature as it must first be determined by citizens whether hacking the government, for the purposes stated, is a legitimate form of Neo-revolutionary political action. If the answer to this question is yes, then debate and discussion needs to immediately begin on what this would look like.

The founding revolutionaries of America sincerely believed in government of the people by the people. For them, merely possessing the right to vote was not the beginning and end of their rights nor of their civic duties as Americans. They viewed government as a servant of the people. Government exists to carry out the will of its citizens, not to act as parasites on the rights guaranteed under the United States Constitution and the laws of the nation. No amount of sport and play today would distract them away from personally remedying the abuses that presently acceptable as inevitable.

Nothing written in this book will be of any interest to the citizen who is a sleep walker. The citizen who can't imagine a government that does not have the right to arbitrarily invade citizens' privacy, will unwittingly wave this off and return to their routine diversions of the day. Dropping a vote into the ballot box is the extent of their interest and commitment to the affairs of this nation. They believe that this is all freedom requires. Oh, that that were the case! Though this perspective be poor and bereft of the appreciation for those early revolutionary Americans, it is nonetheless their prerogative to think and act in this manner.

On the other hand, for those Americans who believe that tending to matters of statehood is the epitome of civic duty, there is much to be debated, decided and done. May this process be inspirational, rational and result in a solution to these two critical problems that threaten America from within. Millions of lives, domestically and abroad, will be impacted for decades to come by what is decide today…

www.ingramcontent.com/pod-product-compliance
Lightning Source LLC
Chambersburg PA
CBHW031326250726
48656CB00005B/1998